IN FOCUS...

HOW DINOSAURS LIVED

Dougal Dixon

Quarto Library

Quarto is the authority on a wide range of topics.
Quarto educates, entertains and enriches the lives of our readers—enthusiasts and lovers of hands-on living.
www.quartoknows.com

This library edition published in 2020
by Quarto Library,
an imprint of The Quarto Group.
26391 Crown Valley Parkway,
Suite 220
Mission Viejo, CA 92691, USA
T: +1 949 380 7510
F: +1 949 380 7575
www.QuartoKnows.com

Distributed in the United States and Canada by
Lerner Publisher Services
241 First Avenue North
Minneapolis, MN 55401 U.S.A.
www.lernerbooks.com

A CIP record for this book is available from the Library of Congress.

ISBN: 978 0 7112 4811 3

Manufactured in Guangdong, China CC042020

9 8 7 6 5 4 3 2 1

FSC www.fsc.org
MIX
Paper from responsible sources
FSC® C008047

CONTENTS

Words in **bold** are explained in the Glossary on page 31.

THE WORLD OF DINOSAURS

Long before there were people on Earth, mighty dinosaurs ruled the planet. Dinosaurs and other amazing **reptiles** were the main animals on Earth for 150 million years. These creatures lived in the ancient seas, skies, and on the land.

Discovering dinosaurs

Most dinosaurs became **extinct** 66 million years ago. This means that paleontologists, or scientists that study dinosaurs, have to figure out what they were like by looking at dinosaur **fossils**. They fit together pieces such as bones and teeth to work out what a dinosaur looked like. This can also tell us other things, such as what the dinosaurs ate, how they moved, and when they lived.

Many dinosaurs had thick, pebbly skin, but some had scales like modern reptiles.

Great and small

Dinosaurs came in all shapes and sizes. The biggest were more than 100 feet (30 meters) long. These giants were some of the largest creatures that ever lived. Other dinosaurs were tiny and looked a bit like birds. There are more than 1,000 dinosaurs that we know about.

The group of dinosaurs called dromaeosaurs had razor-sharp claws and teeth for killing their prey.

The gentle giants known as sauropods lumbered along on all fours and ate only plants.

DINO DATA

The word dinosaur means "terrible lizard." Dinosaurs were given this name by English scientist Richard Owen in 1842.

TYPES OF DINOSAUR

Some theropods had big heads and jaws lined with razor-sharp teeth.

Scientists split dinosaurs into two groups, or "orders." The main difference between these groups was their hip bones. The saurischian dinosaurs were "lizard-hipped." The ornithischian dinosaurs were "bird-hipped."

Lizard-hipped dinosaurs

The group of lizard-hipped dinosaurs included both meat-eating and plant-eating animals. The meat-eating group, called the **theropods**, ranged from huge monsters such as *Tyrannosaurus*, down to small, scampering hunters such as *Compsognathus*, who were no bigger than chickens. Huge, plant-eating sauropods such as *Apatosaurus* and *Diplodocus* were also lizard-hipped dinosaurs.

DINO DATA

The lizard-hipped dromaeosaurs had a lethal claw on each foot, which they used as deadly weapons.

Dinosaurs' legs were straight beneath their bodies instead of sprawled out to one side like early reptiles.

Bird-hipped dinosaurs

The bird-hipped dinosaurs were all plant-eaters. Like the lizard-hipped dinosaurs, these animals came in many different shapes and sizes. The boneheaded and duckbilled dinosaurs usually walked on their two back legs. Armored dinosaurs such as *Ankylosaurus* had bony armor on their backs for protection. This group also included the spiky **stegosaurs** and the horned dinosaurs such as *Triceratops*.

DINOSAUR DIETS

Some of the most famous dinosaurs are the killer meat-eaters, such as *Tyrannosaurus*. But in fact there were many more plant-eating animals than meat-eaters in the **prehistoric** world.

Plant-eaters

Big plant-eaters such as the sauropods could reach the tops of trees. They tore the leaves off branches with their strong teeth. They swallowed mouthfuls of leaves whole because they could not chew properly. Smaller plant-eaters munched on leaves from lower branches, or plants that grew on the ground, such as ferns.

The large sauropods used their long necks to reach fresh leaves at the tops of trees.

Meat-eaters

Only the largest hunters would have dared attack the biggest plant-eaters. Even then, they would probably have chosen a young or injured animal to attack. Smaller meat-eaters probably caught lizards and insects for most of their food. Some dinosaurs hunted in packs to bring down creatures much larger than themselves.

Ornitholestes ate lizards and frogs, as well as insects and early birds.

DINO DATA

Many plant-eating dinosaurs swallowed small rocks, which helped mush up the tough plant matter in their stomachs.

TYRANT LIZARDS

The tyrannosaurs were some of the largest meat-eaters ever. They thundered across Earth, terrorizing their prey. Their name means "tyrant lizards."

The first tyrannosaur

The first known tyrannosaur was *Guanlong*. It lived about 100 million years before *Tyrannosaurus*. *Guanlong's* arms were longer than the arms of later tyrannosaurs and it was the size of a dog. It also had three fingers on each hand instead of two. The remains of two *Guanlong* were found together in China.

Albertosaurus had a big head and a short body, balancing on strong, pillar-like legs.

Late developers

Tyrannosaurus and its large relatives only roamed the planet for a few million years. This is a short amount of time compared to many dinosaurs. The tyrannosaurs died out 66 million years ago.

Tarbosaurus lived in Asia in the late **Cretaceous period**. Fossils of this dinosaur have been found in Mongolia.

Hunters or scavengers?

All tyrannosaurs had huge heads, strong legs, and tiny arms. They looked ferocious, but their size might have been a problem when hunting. Their bulky bodies made it hard to chase prey. They probably preferred to look for dead animals to eat.

DINO DATA

Young tyrannosaurs may have been covered in feathers, which dropped off as they got older.

BIRDLIKE DINOSAURS

Scientists believe that birds evolved from a group of small dinosaurs called dromaeosaurs. Their name means "running lizards," and these animals could run upright on their long, slim back legs. The ornithomimids were another group of birdlike dinosaurs.

Struthiomimus had long arms and strong, curved claws.

Runners

Open **plains** encourage the evolution of long-legged, high-headed running animals—all the better for seeing danger coming from a long way away and escaping from it. The ornithomimids evolved an appearance and a lifestyle like modern ostriches.

Life on the plains

Ornithomimids were fast movers. Some of them could reach speeds of nearly 40 miles (64 kilometers) per hour. They lived on the plains of North America and traveled in **herds**.

DINO DATA

Raptors had a large, curved claw on the second toe of each foot. This might have helped them climb, as well as kill their prey.

A pair of *Velociraptors* patrol the shore of an ancient lake looking for their next meal.

Therizinosaurus was related to the raptors. It had huge claws and a toothless mouth.

Dromaeosaurs

Dromaeosaurs are sometimes called "raptors." Although they were not big animals, they were fierce **predators**. They were probably the most intelligent dinosaurs ever to roam Earth. The dromaeosaurs were covered in feathers.

PACK HUNTERS

When the remains of meat-eating dinosaurs were first found, they were usually on their own. This made scientists think that dinosaurs were lone hunters. This theory changed as more fossils were discovered.

Fossil evidence

Deinonychus was a close relative of *Velociraptor*. The remains of more than one *Deinonychus* were found in the same place. They were close to the skeleton of a plant-eating *Tenontosaurus*. This discovery suggests that *Deinonychus* hunted its prey in packs.

Deinonychus could kill prey with the large, curved claws on its feet.

Pack attack

It was probably smaller hunting dinosaurs that attacked in packs. The clever dromaeosaurs may have worked together to bring down large plant-eaters. A group of predators would surround their victim. Some leaped onto its back, while others slashed its skin with their sharp claws.

Velociraptor hunted in packs. This meant it could hunt much bigger dinosaurs than itself.

By working togather, hunters could kill even large dinosaurs such as sauropods.

DINO DATA

Pack hunters would chase down their victim like hunting dogs, before making the final pounce.

KILLER GIANTS

The "lizard-hipped" dinosaurs are divided into two smaller groups—theropods and sauropods. The theropods were flesh-eating predators that walked on their back legs, including big beasts such as *Allosaurus* and *Tyrannosaurus*.

A family of horned *Torosaurus* guarding its nest against the huge theropod *Tyrannosaurus* and the little theropod *Acheroraptor*.

Deadly hunters

Many theropods were speedy runners that could easily catch their slower-moving, plant-eating prey. Their birdlike feet had sharp claws for holding onto flesh. As the theropods evolved, they became bigger, sharper-eyed, and more intelligent.

DINO DATA

Although their feet were similar to birds' feet, the word theropod actually means "beast-footed."

Dilophosaurus was an active hunter. It had a double **crest** on its head.

The true monsters

The largest theropods include *Carcharodontosaurus* and *Giganotosaurus*. Some of these giants could grow to nearly 60 feet (18 meters) long. This was much bigger than *Tyrannosaurus*.

Tiny theropods

Not all theropods were huge. *Compsognathus* was about the size of a turkey. Its bones were hollow, so it was very light. This made it a fast hunter. *Parvicursor* was even smaller. This tiny dinosaur was only 15 inches (38 centimeters) from nose to tail.

Little *Compsognathus* had a long neck and tail to help it balance while running.

MASSIVE MEAT-EATERS

The allosaurs and the spinosaurs were among the largest meat-eaters in the prehistoric world. These animals lived from the **Jurassic period** to the Cretaceous. They lumbered across every **continent** in the world.

Allosaurs

The giant allosaurs had large heads on short, strong necks. In front of their eyes were two small, bony lumps. Allosaurs used their heavy tails to balance. Their short arms ended in three-clawed hands. Despite their size, allosaurs may have hunted in packs.

Allosaurus teeth marks have been found in the fossil of another dinosaur, evidence of an attack by this giant meat-eater.

DINO DATA

Spinosaurus's *long, crocodile-like jaw was ideal for reaching inside dead dinosaurs to feed.*

Suchomimus may have walked on all fours sometimes, to support its heavy body.

Spinosaurs

Spinosaurs, such as *Suchomimus*, were also huge meat-eating dinosaurs, but they had a more unusual appearance. Some of them had backbones that grew outward to form a "**sail**" down their backs, similar to the sails on pelycosaurs, such as *Dimetrodon*. The sail may have helped them to warm up or cool down.

Suchomimus had three huge, sharp claws on each hand, which it may have used to grip its prey.

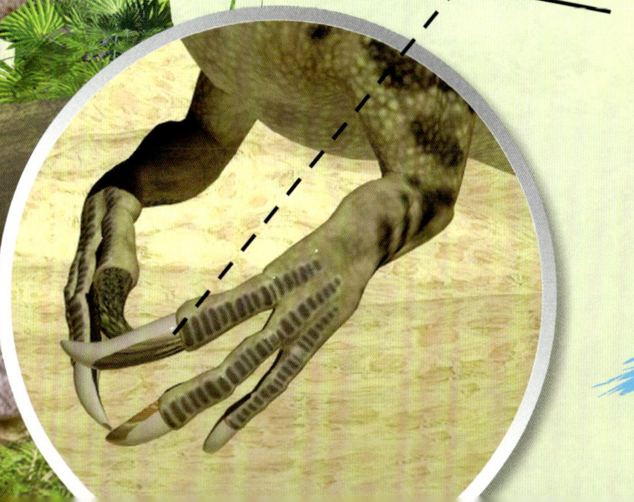

SPINOSAURUS

Scientists used to think that *Tyrannosaurus* was the biggest of the meat-eating dinosaurs. It has since been found that others, such as *Spinosaurus*, were much longer. The 50-foot (15-meter) long *Spinosaurus* was one of a group of strange, fish-eating dinosaurs that existed all over the world in early Cretaceous times.

DINO DATA

Spinosaurs have been found in England, Morocco, Egypt, Thailand, and Brazil.

Like all spinosaurs, *Baryonyx* had long, narrow crocodile-like jaws, full of sharp, pointed teeth for seizing slippery prey.

A fishy diet

The first complete spinosaur to be found was *Baryonyx*. It was obviously a fish-catching animal—not only did it have fish-catching teeth, but there were fish scales and bones found in the stomach of its skeleton. A big claw on each hand was used for hooking fish out of the water.

The sailbacks

Most of the spinosaurs that have been discovered had spectacular sails on their backs. These sails were supported by spines jutting upward from the backbones—hence the name of the group. On some, the sail was merely a ridge along the back, but on others, like that on *Spinosaurus* itself, it was huge. *Ichthyovenator* had two sails.

LIVING IN A HERD

DINO DATA

Bones have been found of a herd of Maiasaura. They suggest that there may have been 10,000 dinosaurs in the herd!

The fossil footprints of dinosaurs and other prehistoric animals offer clues about how they lived. Lots of footprints from the same type of dinosaur have been found together. These suggest that plant-eating dinosaurs lived in herds.

Today, animals such as musk oxen protect their young by circling them, like these *Triceratops* may have done.

Horned herds

Horned dinosaurs such as *Triceratops* might have lived in herds. They defended their babies by forming a circle around them and threatening the predator with their fierce horns.

Gathering information

Fossil footprints tell us many things about dinosaurs. By studying them, scientists can figure out whether a dinosaur ran on four legs or two, how wide its body was, and even how fast it was traveling.

Even the giant sauropods may have moved in herds for safety.

Herds of dinosaurs often left footprints in the mud around rivers and lakes.

How fossil footprints form

Imagine that a herd of dinosaurs gathers near a river or lake. They leave their footprints in the mud. These are baked hard into the Earth by the beating Sun, and later the prints are covered over by more mud. Millions of years later, the prints reappear, as the surface of the land wears away.

ATTACK AND DEFENSE

Life in the prehistoric world was all about survival. For the meat-eaters, this meant being able to catch and kill other animals. Plant-eating dinosaurs had to travel around in search of **vegetation** to eat, but they also had to defend themselves against attack.

DINO DATA

Many smaller dinosaurs relied only on their speed to escape from attackers!

A spiky body made it difficult for even much larger dinosaurs to kill the armored ankylosaurs.

Catching prey

Meat-eating dinosaurs had vicious claws and teeth to attack their prey, but it was not always easy to catch another dinosaur. Some meat-eaters would chase down a plant-eater, but slower-moving animals probably hid among trees and ambushed their victims.

Styracosaurus had huge horns as weapons, and an enormous neck frill for protection.

On the defensive

To make it harder for meat-eaters to kill them, many plant-eating dinosaurs had special body features. Some had bony plates like armor on their backs. Others had horns on their heads or snouts, or spikes on their bodies and tails.

Size matters

The sauropods' great size may have put off many predators. If they were attacked, sauropods may have used their long, strong tails to lash out at their attacker.

Some sauropods, such as *Camarasaurus*, may have had **quills** for extra protection against predators.

FAMILY LIFE

Scientists study fossils and look at the habits of modern animals to find out how dinosaurs behaved. One area of dinosaur behavior is how different species cared for their young.

Most eggs left in a nest would be eaten by predators.

Dinosaur eggs

Like most other reptiles, dinosaurs laid eggs. Different species laid different numbers of eggs. Some types may have laid up to 30 eggs at a time. In the harsh prehistoric world though, only a few baby dinosaurs would have survived.

Safety in numbers

It was easy for predators to attack young dinosaurs, even big baby sauropods. For safety, plant-eaters moved in herds. The young dinosaurs would travel in the middle of the herd.

Young sauropods may have put on as much weight as 7 pounds (3 kilograms) every day!

DINO DATA

Dinosaur eggs weren't as big as you might think. The eggs of giant sauropods were smaller than a bowling ball.

Caring for young

Certain types of dinosaurs seem to have taken great care of their babies. They would feed and watch over them in the nest, like mother birds do today. Other dinosaurs probably laid their eggs and then left them. If they survived long enough to hatch, the young dinosaurs had to fend for themselves.

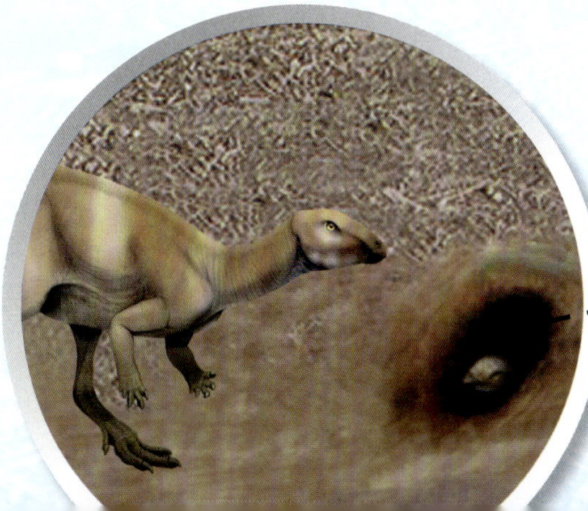

Some dinosaurs may have dug burrows under the ground to keep their young safe.

THE FIRST BIRDS

No one knows for sure how and when the first birds evolved, but they probably evolved from theropod dinosaurs during the Jurassic period. *Archaeopteryx*, which had bird-like bones, wings, and feathers, is often called the "first bird."

DINO DATA

Birds use their feathers as a display to attract a mate. It's believed dinosaurs may have done this, too.

Bird beaks

Fossils of a crow-sized bird named *Confuciusornis* have been found in China. Many of the fossils appear to have long tail feathers. *Confuciusornis* lived around 125 million years ago and, like modern birds, it had a toothless beak.

Fossils of the early bird *Protopteryx* have been found in China.

Feathers

The first feathers may have made a fluffy layer that helped keep dinosaurs warm. As birds evolved, their feathers could be used for flight and to display to mates.

Confuciusornis had claws on its wings and provides a strong link between dinosaurs and birds today.

New findings

Scientists identify about 50 new types of dinosaur every year, and make exciting discoveries about how they lived. They can even work out the color of fossilized feathers, but there is much more to learn.

PICTURE CREDITS

Key: FC = front cover, BC = back cover, t = top, b = bottom, c = center, r = right, l = left.

Alamy:
12-13 Stocktrek Images Inc; 16-17 Stocktrek Images Inc.

All Canada Photos:
6-7 MasPix.

Beehive Illustration:
2 Leonello Calvetti y Luca Messini; 22-23 Leonello Calvetti y Luca Messini, 23tr Leonello Calvetti y Luca Messini; 25b, Leonello Calvetti y Luca Messini; 26-27 Leonello Calvetti y Luca Messini; 28-29 Lazlo Veres.

Dreamstime:
4-5 Linda Bucklin; 6cl Valentyna Chukhlyebova, 7cr 3dalia; 9cr Linda Bucklin; 14-15 Corey A. Ford; 17tr Mr1805, 17br Linda Bucklin; 30 Linda Bucklin.

Getty Images:
10br Dorling Kindersley; 13br Sergey Krasovskiy; 20bl Yuriy Priymak/Corbis/Stocktrek Images, 20-21 Mark Stevenson/Corbis/Stocktrek Images; 24-25 Yuriy Priymak/Stocktrek Images.

Natural History Museum:
27b Andrey Atuchin / The Trustees of the Natural History Museum, London.

Photo Library:
23br Andoni Canela.

Science Photo Library:
14bc Roger Harris, 15cr Jose Antonio Peñas.

Shutterstock:
FC Linda Bucklin; BC Computer Earth; 5tl Michael Rosskothen; 10-11 DM7; 19tr Konstyantyn Ivanyshen, 19br Konstyantyn Ivanyshen; 21tr Michael Rosskothen; 25tr DM7; 28cr Bob Ainsworth.

The publisher gratefully acknowledges the permission granted to reproduce the copyright material in this book. Every effort has been made to trace copyright holders and to obtain their permission for the use of copyright material. The publisher apologizes for any errors or omissions in the above list and would be grateful if notified of any corrections that should be incorporated in future reprints or editions of this book.

GLOSSARY

continent
a very large area of land surrounded by ocean

crest
a raised area or ridge on top of the head; some animals have crests of colorful feathers

Cretaceous period
a period of time in Earth's history that lasted from 145 million years ago to 66 million years ago

extinct
there are no members of this type, or species, of animal still alive

fossil
the remains of a long-dead animal or plant that have, over time, been turned into stone

herd
a group of plant-eating animals that live together

Jurassic period
a period of time in Earth's history that lasted from 200 million years ago to 145 million years ago

plains
large, flat areas of land with few trees

predator
an animal that hunts other animals to eat

prehistoric
describes a time long before humans lived on Earth, or could write about their world

prey
an animal that is hunted by other animals for food

quill
a sharp spine or a long, stiff feather

reptile
a scaly-skinned animal; most reptiles lay their eggs on land, although some reptiles give birth instead

sail
a large, fin-like structure on the back of some prehistoric reptiles

sauropods
large plant-eating dinosaurs with four large legs, a long neck, and small head

stegosaurs
four-legged dinosaurs that had small heads and a double row of bony plates or spines along the back; stegosaurs ate plants

theropods
meat-eating dinosaurs that usually walked on two legs

vegetation
a collection of plants found in one place

INDEX